DATE DUE			

15323

629.228
COO

Cook, Nick.

The world's fastest
cars

Built for Speed

The World's Fastest Cars

by Nick Cook

Consultant:
Anthony Vestal
Media Communications Manager
National Hot Rod Association

CAPSTONE BOOKS

an imprint of Capstone Press
Mankato, Minnesota

Capstone Books are published by Capstone Press
151 Good Counsel Drive, P.O. Box 669, Mankato, Minnesota 56002
http://www.capstone-press.com

Library of Congress Cataloging-in-Publication Data

Cook, Nick.
    The world's fastest cars/by Nick Cook.
    p. cm.—(Built for speed)
    Includes bibliographical references and index.
    Summary: Discusses the history and development of some of the world's fastest
automobiles, describing the specific features and specifications of such cars as
dragsters, Indianapolis 500 race cars, and the supersonic car.
    ISBN 0-7368-0570-2
    1. Automobiles, Racing—Juvenile literature. [1. Automobiles, Racing.
2. Automobile racing.] I. Title. II. Built for speed (Mankato, Minn.)

TL236 .C593 2001
629.228—dc21   00-027505

Editorial Credits
Blake Hoena, editor; Timothy Halldin, cover designer and illustrator; Erin Scott, Sarin
    Creative, illustrator; Katy Kudela, photo researcher

Photo Credits
AP/Wide World Sports, 22, 38 (bottom), 39 (top)
Bruce McLaren Trust, 10
Jon Eisberg/FPG International LLC, 16, 21
Louise Ann Noeth, cover, 4, 7, 30, 33, 35, 39 (bottom), 40, 42
Photo Network/David A. Jentz, 18; Mark Sherman, 27, 29
Ron Kimball/Ron Kimball Studios, 9, 13, 38 (top)
Unicorn Stock Photos/Rod Furgason, 24

Table of Contents

Chapter 1

Fast Cars

In the late 1700s, inventors built the first cars. Since then, people have designed cars to travel at faster and faster speeds.

The earliest speed records were set in the late 1800s. On December 18, 1898, Gaston de Chasseloup-Laubat of France set the first automotive speed record. He reached a speed of 39.24 miles (63.15 kilometers) per hour with an electric car. A month later, Camille Janatzy of Belgium set a new record. He drove his electric car 41.42 miles (66.66 kilometers) per hour.

People continued to set new speed records. In 1904, Frenchman Louis Rigolly drove faster than 100 miles (160 kilometers) per hour. Henry Segrave reached a speed of more than 200 miles

---

Many cars have been designed to travel at fast speeds.

(322 kilometers) per hour in 1927. In 1964, Craig Breedlove drove his car faster than 500 miles (805 kilometers) per hour. Richard Noble set a record speed of 633 miles (1,019 kilometers) per hour in 1983.

In October 1997, Andy Green set the world's fastest car speed record. He reached an average speed of 763 miles (1,228 kilometers) per hour in a jet-powered car. This car is called the Thrust Supersonic Car (SSC).

Types of Fast Cars

Over the years, several types of cars have been designed to reach fast speeds. Automobile companies have built some of these cars. Many auto companies produce high-performance sports cars for the public to buy. These production cars are designed to handle well at high speeds. Currently, the McLaren F1 is the world's fastest production car.

Race cars are designed for high speeds. Some race cars compete on short, straight stretches of track. These cars include Top Fuel dragsters. Others are designed to race many laps around

Race cars are built to reach fast speeds.

longer racetracks. These cars include Formula 1
Indy cars.

Some car designers build or modify cars in
order to set speed records. For example,
designers built the Thrust SSC to break the
sound barrier. They hoped that the Thrust SSC
could travel faster than the speed of sound.
Sound travels at about 760 miles (1,200
kilometers) per hour. The speed of sound varies
depending on altitude and the air's temperature.

Features

Fast cars have three common elements. These include powerful engines, lightweight body parts, and aerodynamic designs. These designs reduce wind resistance. This force slows down moving objects.

An engine's power is measured in horsepower. One horsepower is the force needed to move 33,000 pounds (14,969 kilograms) 1 foot (30 centimeters) in 1 minute. Cars with more powerful engines often can travel at higher speeds than cars with less powerful engines.

Fast cars also need lightweight parts. Heavier cars need more force to move them. Fast cars' parts often are made from magnesium, carbon fiber, and aluminum. These materials are strong and lightweight.

Fast cars need an aerodynamic design to allow air to flow smoothly over and around them. Wind resistance increases with an object's speed. This air force opposes movement.

Costs

Fast cars are expensive to build and operate. They often require special fuel, equipment, and parts. Other costs may include insurance, replacement

An aerodynamic design helps lessen wind resistance.

parts, and mechanics' salaries. These costs can amount to millions of dollars.

Many racers have sponsors to help pay for operating costs. A sponsor can be a person or a company. Sponsor companies often make automobile parts or equipment. Sponsors' names and logos are placed on racers' cars and clothing. In return, sponsors may pay racers or give them equipment to use. Racers often receive an award of money from sponsors when they do well in a race.

Chapter 2

McLaren F1

The McLaren F1 is the fastest production car. The McLaren Car company built only 100 of these cars. The McLaren F1 sells for about $800,000.

From the Track to the Street

Bruce McLaren was a race car driver during the 1950s and 1960s. He won two Formula 1 championships, five Canadian-American sports car championships, and three Indy 500 races. In 1964, McLaren helped form the Bruce McLaren Motor Racing company. This company began to build race cars.

In 1970, McLaren died in a crash while testing a new car design. But his company continued to build race cars. In 1989, the

Racecar driver Bruce McLaren helped form the Bruce McLaren Motor Racing company.

McLaren Car company began to design and sell production cars.

Powerful Engine

An engine's size and the number of cylinders it has help determine how much power it produces. Cylinders are the spaces in an engine where gasoline is burned to create power. The McLaren Fl's engine is 6.1 liters. This measurement is the volume of all the cylinders. The McLaren F1 has a V-12 engine. This means that it has 12 cylinders set together in pairs that form the shape of a V.

The McLaren F1's engine is powerful. It produces 618 horsepower. The McLaren F1 can go from 0 to 60 miles (97 kilometers) per hour in just 3.4 seconds. It also can reach speeds faster than 200 miles (322 kilometers) per hour.

Lightweight

The McLaren F1 weighs 2,579 pounds (1,170 kilograms). This weight is less than many other sports cars. For example, the Chevrolet Corvette weighs 400 pounds (181 kilograms) more than the McLaren F1.

The McLaren F1 is built from lightweight materials.

The McLaren F1 is built from lightweight materials. The engine block is made from an aluminum alloy and magnesium. The car's chassis and many of its body parts are made from carbon fiber. A car's chassis includes its frame, wheels, axles, and parts that hold the engine in place.

The McLaren F1's designers used body parts that would reduce the car's weight. The compact disc player is a special lightweight model. Designers also did not include a spare tire in order to reduce the car's weight.

Seating

Drivers sit in the middle of the McLaren F1. This seating position is similar to race cars. In this position, the front wheel wells do not interfere with the driver's leg room.

The McLaren F1 has "1-plus-2" seating. In most production cars, the front-seat passenger sits to the right of the driver. In the F1, a passenger's seat is located on each side of the driver. These seats are slightly behind the driver.

Lift

Lift can cause cars to rise off the ground and crash when traveling at high speeds. This air force also helps airplanes fly.

Lift is created by the flow of air over and under a car. Air flows faster over cars than it does under them. Slow-moving air has higher pressure than fast-moving air. High-pressure air moves toward low-pressure air.

The slow-moving air under a car creates high pressure. This high-pressure air then rises

Lift

Fast-moving air over a car
causes low air pressure.

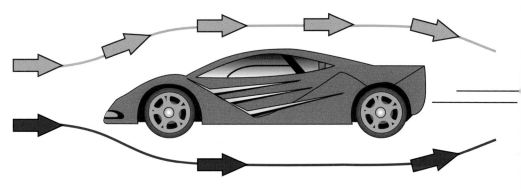

Air moves slower underneath cars. This
movement creates high air pressure.
The high-pressure air rises toward the
low-pressure air. This force is known as lift.

toward the low-pressure air above the car. This force increases as a car's speed increases. Lift can cause cars to flip and crash at high speeds.

Designers worked on decreasing lift under the McLaren F1. They created a large opening at the bottom of the car's nose. The car's rear also has a similar opening. Powerful fans force air through these openings. This creates lower pressure under the car and lessens the lift.

Chapter 3

Indy Cars

The Indy 500 race takes place the last weekend in May. This 500-mile (805-kilometer) race is held at the Indianapolis Motor Speedway in Indiana. Indy cars are designed to race on this racecourse. They are the most powerful Formula 1 race cars. Indy cars can reach speeds of more than 200 miles (322 kilometers) per hour.

Indy 500 History

In 1899, Carl Fisher bought the first automobile sold in Indianapolis. But Fisher did not like the way that cars of the time often broke down.

In 1909, Fisher and three friends built a racetrack. They invited automakers to test the cars that they built on this racetrack.

Indy cars are the most powerful Formula 1 race cars.

Indy cars have wings and side pods.

In 1911, Fisher and his partners held a 500-mile (805-kilometer) race on their track. This was the first Indy 500. Ray Harroun won the race. Harroun's average speed was nearly 75 miles (120 kilometers) per hour.

Chassis and Body

An Indy car's chassis is long and narrow. It is between 190 and 195 inches (483 and 495 centimeters) long. The chassis is made of aluminum and carbon fiber. Indy cars weigh less than 1,550 pounds (703 kilograms).

Racers sit in a cockpit in front of the engine. A six-point seat belt holds them securely in their seat. Racers sit in a reclining position. Their legs extend into the car's nose.

The fuel tank is located behind the driver. It holds 40 gallons (151 liters) of fuel. Indy cars run on methanol instead of gasoline. This fuel is made from alcohol.

Engines

Currently, Indy cars have V-8 engines. These engines can produce between 750 and 900 horsepower. But the engines wear out quickly. Mechanics must rebuild them after each race.

Most Indy car engines have a turbocharger. This device forces extra air into the fuel. Fuel needs air to burn. Extra air helps the engine burn more fuel. This creates more power.

Wings and Side Pods

Indy cars have wings and side pods. These features create downforce. This force prevents lift from raising cars off the ground.

Indy cars have three wings. A short wing is attached to each side of an Indy car's pointed nose. A larger wing is at the car's rear. Air rushes over these wings and pushes down on them. This force increases tire traction. Traction is the gripping power of Indy car tires on pavement when racing at high speeds.

Indy cars have a pod on each side. Side pods hold engine parts and the radiator. Radiators circulate a cooling liquid through the car's engine. The bottom of the pods is curved. Air rushes into these curved pockets and lowers the air pressure. This reduces lift.

Tires

Indy car tires are wide. But the front tires are narrower than the back tires. This makes it easier for drivers to turn.

Racers use two types of tires. They use smooth tires to race during dry days. The entire surface of a smooth tire touches the racetrack. A tire has better traction when more of its surface touches the pavement. Racers use tires with tread on rainy days. These tires have grooves that help remove water from between the pavement and the tire's surface. Water could cause the tires to lose traction.

Racers use smooth tires to race on dry racetracks.

Arie Luyendyk

Luyendyk was born September 21, 1953, in Sommelsdyk, the Netherlands. His father raced and repaired cars. Luyendyk often accompanied his father to races. Luyendyk began his racing career at a Dutch driving school. In 1972, he began to race small European road-racing vehicles. He won the Dutch Firestone Formula Ford Championship in 1973. In 1983, he moved to the United States to pursue a racing career. A year later, he raced his first Indy car at Elkhart Lake's Road America. He placed eighth in this race. In 1985, he placed seventh in his first Indy 500 race. In 1987, he finished in the top 10 in nine races. Because of this success, his fellow race car drivers voted him the "Most Improved Driver" of 1987. He won the Indy 500 in 1990 and 1997.

Smart Cars

Indy cars contain computers. These computers are connected to sensors. Sensors check cars' performance during a race. They measure cars' speed, oil pressure, and horsepower.

A racer's pit crew monitors this information. These mechanics carefully watch the car's data. They then can adjust the car's performance or warn the driver of potential trouble.

Safety Features

Safety is important at high speeds. A crash could seriously injure or kill a racer.

Indy cars have roll bars. These steel bars are located behind the racer's seat. Roll bars protect racers if their car flips over.

Indy car cockpits are built for safety. The seat and steering wheel have heavy padding. The nose has a metal plate inside it. This plate protects a racer's feet during a head-on collision.

Racers wear safety clothing. These clothes are made from a fire-resistant material called Nomex. This material protects racers in case of fire during a race or accident. Racers' suits, gloves, shoes, socks, and underwear are made of Nomex.

Chapter 4

Top Fuel Dragsters

Dragsters are raced on short, straight stretches of road. These tracks are one-fourth of a mile (400 meters) long. Drag racers can race several types of dragsters. But Top Fuel dragsters are the fastest. They can reach speeds of 300 miles (483 kilometers) per hour in less than 5 seconds.

Street Races

Drag racing began in southern California in the 1940s. Racers modified production cars' engines to make them more powerful. They then raced these cars on streets, dry lake beds, airport runways, or in deserts. Racers called these cars hot rods. But this type of racing was illegal and dangerous. Races did not have any safety rules.

Top Fuel dragsters can reach speeds of 300 miles (483 kilometers) per hour.

In 1950, the first organized drag race took place in Santa Ana, California. In 1951, racers formed the National Hot Rod Association (NHRA). This organization sets the rules for drag racing. Today, the NHRA sanctions drag racing events throughout the United States. These races follow NHRA rules and guidelines.

The Racing V

Top Fuel dragsters sometimes are called "slingshots" or "rails." These cars look very different from production cars. The chassis of a Top Fuel dragster forms a long, narrow V. These cars can be as long as 25 feet (7.6 meters).

Top Fuel dragsters are lightweight. They weigh about half as much as most production cars. Much of a Top Fuel dragster's weight is in the rear. The engine is located in the rear. The weight increases the back tires' traction.

Top Fuel dragsters use special fuels. They burn a mixture of nitromethane and alcohol. Nitromethane also is used to fuel rockets. This fuel mixture can increase an engine's power by

Top Fuel dragsters' engines are located behind the racer.

50 percent. Top Fuel dragster engines can produce more than 6,000 horsepower.

Traction

Top Fuel dragsters' front and rear tires are not the same size. The front tires are smaller and narrower than the rear tires. The rear tires are called slicks because they are smooth and have no tread. They are nearly 3 feet (.9 meters) wide. Their width and lack of tread give these tires a great deal of traction.

Top Fuel dragsters also have a large rear wing. The airflow over this wing creates downforce. The downforce increases the rear tires' traction.

Fast Stops and Safety

Top Fuel dragsters have brakes similar to production cars. But these brakes are not powerful enough to stop Top Fuel dragsters at high speeds.

Dragsters that reach speeds greater than 150 miles (241 kilometers) per hour use parachutes to stop. These lightweight pieces of strong fabric are folded into a small pack at the car's rear. Racers yank a release cord at the end of the race to open the parachute. The parachute then opens and quickly slows down the car.

Driver safety is important. Dragster cockpits have roll bars. The space behind the head of the racer is heavily padded. Racers wear Nomex suits. They also wear goggles, gloves, and a helmet for protection.

Top Fuel dragsters use parachutes to stop.

Chapter 5

Thrust SSC

Richard Noble set an automotive speed record of 633 miles (1,019 kilometers) per hour in 1983. But Noble wanted to set one more speed record. He wanted to break the sound barrier with a car. Vehicles that travel faster than the speed of sound are called supersonic. Noble named his car the Thrust Supersonic Car (SSC).

Testing

Noble asked Ron Ayers for help in designing the Thrust SSC. Ayers is an aerodynamicist. He studies how the forces of air affect objects that are in motion.

At first, Ayers did not believe that a car could break the sound barrier. Vehicles that break the sound barrier create shock waves. Many people

Richard Noble hoped to design a car that could break the sound barrier.

believed that these shock waves would cause a car to crash. But Ayers agreed to research the possibility of designing such a car.

Ayers designed a model of the Thrust SSC on a computer used to test supersonic planes. The computer then simulated a supersonic run for the car. The results of this test convinced Ayers that a car could break the sound barrier.

Next, Ayers had a small model of the car built. Testers placed this model on a rocket sled. Rocket engines then pushed the model down a test track at supersonic speeds. Sensors read air pressure around the model. Ayers performed 13 test runs on the model. Results of these tests convinced Ayers and Noble that their car design could safely break the sound barrier. Noble then hired G-Force Engineering in Fontwell, England, to build the car.

Jet Power

The Thrust SSC designers decided to use jet engines to power the car. Jet engines mostly are used in jet airplanes. They operate by sucking air into the engine. Fans inside the engine then push the air into a compressor. The compressor compacts the air. The compressed air then mixes

The Thrust SSC was powered by jet engines.

with fuel and ignites. This creates hot, burning gases. The gases' temperature causes them to expand and rush out the rear of the engine. The force of the moving gases pushes the vehicle forward.

The Thrust SSC is the first land vehicle to use two jet engines. Together, these engines produce 100,000 horsepower.

Staying on the Ground

The Thrust SSC's speed creates a great deal of lift. The car's size helps keep it on the ground.

The Thrust SSC is 54 feet (16 meters) long and 12 feet (3.7 meters) wide. It weighs 20,000 pounds (9,072 kilograms).

The jet engines are the heaviest part of the car. These engines are located on the sides of the car's body. Designers believed that an engine on each side of the car would improve stability at high speeds. They also placed the engines toward the car's front. The engines' weight helped to keep the car's nose down.

An airplane-like tail is located on the car's rear. Air moving over this tail does two things. It helps make the car easier to steer. It also provides downforce to keep the car on the ground.

Shock Waves

Vehicles create intense shock waves when they break the sound barrier. These waves bounce off the ground under the car. They could flip the car.

The Thrust SSC's body is designed to resist shock waves. Its body looks like a fighter jet without wings. The curves and angles of the car's body help scatter the waves harmlessly under the car.

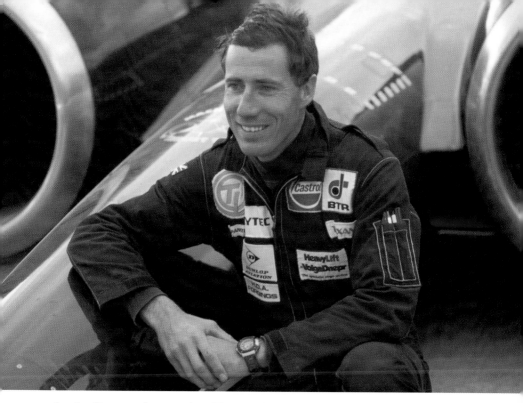

Andy Green drove the Thrust SSC.

Breaking the Sound Barrier

Noble hired Andy Green to drive the Thrust
SSC. Green is a fighter pilot in Great Britain's
Royal Air Force. He has flown supersonic
jet airplanes.

The Thrust SSC team made several attempts at
setting a new speed record. In early September
1997, the Thrust SSC reached the fastest speed
for any land vehicle. This speed was 719 miles
(1,157 kilometers) per hour. But this speed failed

to set a new record. International land speed rules state that a second run must occur within one hour of the first run. These two runs then are averaged to determine a car's speed. The Thrust SSC team failed to make a second run within one hour after its first run.

On September 25, 1997, Green drove the Thrust SSC to a new speed record. The car reached an average speed of 714 miles (1,149 kilometers) per hour. But the Thrust SSC team still hoped to break the sound barrier.

On October 13, 1997, the team reached its goal. Green drove the Thrust SSC to a speed of 764 miles (1,230 kilometers) per hour. This speed broke the sound barrier. But the Thrust SSC team failed to set a new speed record. The second run occurred 61 minutes after the first run.

On October 15, 1997, the Thrust SSC finally set a supersonic speed record. The Thrust SSC team completed two runs within one hour. Green recorded an average speed of 763 miles (1,228 kilometers) per hour.

Sound Barrier

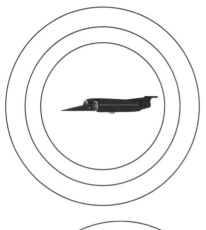

Sound travels in waves. This is similar to when a rock is thrown into water. The sound waves ripple outward like the water. Sound waves surround noisy objects such as fast planes or cars.

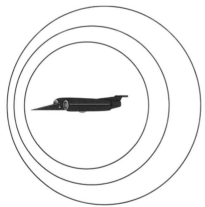

A supersonic car catches up to the sound waves it creates as its speed increases. These waves then pile up in front of the car.

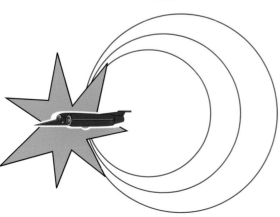

Air pressure increases as the sound waves pile up. This pressure is the sound barrier. The car crashes through the sound barrier when its speed is greater than the speed of sound. This action creates a loud noise called a sonic boom.

FAST FACTS

MCLAREN F1

Driver: Andy Wallace
Record Date: March 31, 1998
Record Speed: 240.14 miles
(386.45
kilometers) per hour
Location: Ehra-Lessien, Germany

INDY CAR

Driver: Arie Luyendyk
Record Date: May 27, 1990
Record Average Speed: 185.981
miles
(299.29
kilometers)
per hour
Location: Indy 500 Motor
Speedway, Indianapolis,
Indiana

TOP FUEL DRAGSTER

Driver: Tony Schumacher
Record Date: January 17, 1999
Record Speed: 330.23 miles
(531.44
kilometers)
per hour
Location: Firebird International
Raceway, Phoenix,
Arizona

THRUST SSC

Driver: Andy Green
Record Date: October 15, 1997
Record Speed: 763.035 miles
(1,227.95
kilometers)
per hour
Location: Black Rock Desert,
Nevada

Chapter 6

Future of
Fast Cars

Cars' speeds have increased greatly over the years. The first cars built in the 1700s traveled at only 3 miles (4.8 kilometers) per hour. Today, technological advances allow designers to build cars that reach speeds greater than 500 miles (805 kilometers) per hour.

Electronics
In the 1960s, cars had simple computers. These computers only controlled a car's fuel injection system. This system pumps gas into a car's engine. Today, complex computers control many engine functions. These computers are called engine control units (ECUs).

Cars' speeds have greatly increased over the years.

Craig Breedlove hopes Spirit of America will be able to break the land speed record.

An ECU is programmed to make adjustments to increase a car's performance. For example, an ECU adjusts the amount of fuel an engine burns. This increases its horsepower. An ECU even can help prevent a car from spinning out of control by controlling the brakes.

Engines

Automakers have made many advancements in car engines. The first cars used electric and steam engines. But these engines could not create enough power to travel at high speeds. In 1876, Nikolaus Otto invented the internal combustion engine that is used in most modern cars today. This engine burns fuel inside the engine.

Today, some auto designers are building cars with jet engines. Craig Breedlove leads the Spirit of America race team. This team's car is powered by a 45,200-horsepower jet engine. It has reached speeds of more than 600 miles (966 kilometers) per hour. Breedlove hopes to break the land speed record with this car.

An Australian team also hopes to break the land speed record. Rosco McGlashan leads the Aussie Invader team. Currently, he holds the Australian speed record at 499 miles (803 kilometers) per hour. His Aussie Invader III car is powered by a 36,000-horsepower jet engine.

Inventors and designers will continue to use technological advances to build faster and more powerful cars. These fast cars may win races and set new speed records. They also will provide exciting entertainment for future car racing fans.

Words to Know

aerodynamic (air-oh-dye-NAM-mik)—designed to cut through the air with little resistance

altitude (AL-ti-tood)—the height of an object above the ground

chassis (CHASS-ee)—the frame, wheels, axles, and parts that hold the engine of a car

horsepower (HORSS-pou-ur)—the measure of an engine's power

methanol (METH-uh-nawl)—a fuel made from alcohol

nitromethane (nye-troh-MEH-thane)—a fuel used to power rockets; nitromethane also can be mixed with gasoline to power cars.

traction (TRAK-shuhn)—friction between an object and the surface it moves on

wind resistance (WIND ri-ZISS-tuhnss)—an air force that opposes the motion of an object; wind resistance increases with an object's speed.

To Learn More

Graham, Ian. *Cars*. Built for Speed. Austin, Texas: Raintree Steck-Vaughn, 1999.

Hintz, Martin, and Kate Hintz. *Top Fuel Drag Racing.* Drag Racing. Mankato, Minn.: Capstone Books, 1996.

Smith, Jay H., *Drag Racing.* MotorSports. Mankato, Minn.: Capstone Books, 1995.

Young, Jesse. *Indy Cars.* Cruisin'. Mankato, Minn.: Capstone Books, 1995.

Useful Addresses

Canadian Automobile Sports Clubs
703 Petrolia Road
Downsview, ON M3J 2N6
Canada

Indianapolis Motor Speedway
4790 West 16th Street
Indianapolis, IN 46222-2573

National Hot Rod Association
2035 Financial Way
Glendora, CA 91741

Sports Car Club of America
9033 East Easter Place
Englewood, CO 80112

Internet Sites

Indianapolis 500
http://www.indy500.com

McLaren Cars Limited
http://www.mclarencars.com

National Hot Rod Association
http://www.nhra.com

Thrust Supersonic Car
http://www.thrustssc.com

Index